The Promised One

For G&P: for all your support and idea bouncing!   A.W.

The original Easter story comes from the Bible. You can find it in all four of the Gospels – Matthew, Mark, Luke, and John.

"He's not here. He has been brought back to life! Remember what he told you while he was still in Galilee. He said, 'The Son of Man must be handed over to sinful people, be crucified, and come back to life on the third day.'"

Text and illustrations copyright © 2017 Antonia Woodward
This edition copyright © 2017 Lion Hudson

The right of Antonia Woodward to be identified as the author of this work has been asserted by her in accordance with the Copyright, Designs and Patents Act 1988.

Published by Lion Children's Books
an imprint of
Lion Hudson plc
Wilkinson House, Jordan Hill Road,
Oxford OX2 8DR, England
www.lionhudson.com/lionchildrens

ISBN 978 0 7459 7679 2

First edition 2017

Acknowledgments
Bible quotations are taken from the Good News Bible © 1994 published by the Bible Societies/HarperCollins Publishers Ltd UK, Good News Bible © American Bible Society 1966, 1971, 1976, 1992. Used with permission.

A catalogue record for this book is available from the British Library

Printed and bound in Serbia, October 2017, LH55

The Promised One

The Wonderful story of Easter

Antonia Woodward

LION
CHILDREN'S

Jesus was making a stir.

He made sick people well.

He made food for thousands

out of almost nothing.

He cared for the lonely and the needy.

He was like no one else, and the people loved him.

At festival time, Jesus rode into the city of Jerusalem on a young donkey. As the crowds saw him coming, they welcomed him with shouts of joy.

"Here comes God-on-earth!" they cheered.

But not everyone was cheering. "Who does he think he is?" the religious leaders grumbled jealously.

When Jesus saw the festival stalls at the Temple, he was frustrated. "You should be here to meet with God, but you are only here to make money. How dare you turn this special place into an ordinary market!"

The religious leaders could stand it no longer. Jesus was showing them up! He had to go.

Now, Jesus had twelve close friends who believed with all their hearts that he was God-on-earth, the Promised One they had been waiting for.

One evening, he told them sadly, "The time is almost here when one of you will turn against me. But remember: these things are all part of God's plan.

"This bread and this wine are to remind you of my body and my blood. When you meet together, think of me as you eat and drink them."

Jesus took three friends to a quiet
garden to pray.

"Father God, I know how terrible the next few days will be
for me. If possible, please change this. But you always know
best, so I will do whatever you ask."

The sound of footsteps and the light of torches interrupted the still darkness.

His close friend Judas was leading the way.

Jesus knew they had come to arrest him.

All night long the religious leaders questioned and accused Jesus. "Are you the promised one? Do you really think you're God-on-earth?"

Finally they marched him to the local ruler, Pilate.

"This man is making trouble," they said. "He claims to be the Son of God. He must be silenced."

"Are you really God-on-earth?" Pilate asked.

But Jesus didn't say a word.

"Take him away," Pilate said at last.

Jesus was led to a hill outside the city, where he was
nailed to a cross.

His friends were devastated. They thought Jesus was the Promised One. They thought he was God-on-earth! How could he let this happen?

But Jesus cried out with a loud voice:

"My task is complete!"

The earth rumbled loudly. The sky went dark.
And Jesus died.

Two days later Jesus' friends went to the tomb where he had been laid. But the heavy stone was rolled aside and Jesus' body was no longer there.

A shining angel was waiting for them.

"You thought this was the end, but it's only the beginning," the angel said. "God always has a plan: Jesus was dead... but he is alive again!"

In the days that followed, Jesus met with many of his friends.
And he told them:

"You thought I had come for you,

in this place,

at this time…

"But God's plans are bigger than you know!

"I came for
everyone,
everywhere,
for all time."

Other titles from Lion Children's Books

The Extra Special Baby Antonia Woodward

The Easter Story Antonia Jackson & Giuliano Ferri
The First Easter Lois Rock & Sophie Allsopp
The Story of Easter Mary Joslin & Alida Massari